Searching For Souls

By: Mikal Bethea

This book or any portion thereof may not be reproduced or used in any manner whatsoever without the express written permission of the publisher except for the use of brief quotations in a book review.

Copyright © 2015 by Mikal Bethea

Editor: Chyna Sallier

First Printing, 2016

ISBN 13: 978-0692710500
ISBN 10: 0692710507

Library of Congress Control Number: 2016941026

BRICKS4 Life Publishing
2 Keer Avenue
#3
Newark, NJ
07112

Website: www.bricks4lifepublishing.com
Facebook: https://www.facebook.com/BRICKS4LifePublishing/?hc_location=ufi

Printed in the United States of America

All rights reserved.

Table of Contents

Acknowledgements 1
Introduction 2
The Woman in the Ocean..3
In Case You Didn't Know...5
Perfect Imperfection 6
My Equation 8
The Mirror of Love..10
Mental Sex..11
I'm Still… You're Still… We're Still…...............................12
The Real You...14
Dreaming 16
The Rose Growing by the Cliff 18
The Single Parent-Mother 19
She's a Brick House 21
The Mirror of Life 23
Broken Promises..25
Acceptance of Self...27
Faith in Self 29
Keep Keeping Your Head Up 31
One In A Million 33
Ms. Independent 35
You Deserve 37
Love is Blind 39
Just Breathe 41
You Already Are 43
The World is yours 45
Superwoman...47
M.O.B 49
Growing Pains 51
Life is What You Make it..52
Be Careful of What You Say 54
You're Only a Woman 56
Push It to the Limit...58
There's a Season for Everything 60
Appreciation of Rain 62

New Life Through Death	64
Traditional Thinking	66
Stand Right There	68
The Caged Birds	70
One Step at a Time	72
When It All Falls Down	74
Exaggeration	76
Torn Between the Two	78
Choices and Consequences	80
What's Best for You	82
Let It Go	84
The Butterfly Effect	86
Tears of Life	88
Alone but not Lonely	90
Waste No Time	92
Jerz-Queen	94
Daddy's Girl – Black Goddess	95
The Mirror	96
Reflection	97
A Message to You	98
Author's Note	99

Acknowledgements

I will first like to acknowledge God, for blessing me with the talent and foresight of understanding to write this book. God knows best! Special thanks to my cousin Shirea, you never gave up on me. To my mom, Emma Bethea, you are my rock; there will never be another you. Special thanks to my good friend and brother Kariem, you play a very important role in me achieving my goals. Let's take it to the next level! There are many others I could name, but this book could never hold them all. So, if I missed your name, blame my mind, not my heart, because it's all love.

Peace, love, and respect,

Mikal

Introduction

To search the soul means to find your inner self. To find that peace and stability many women lack, in your work.

Too many women are drowning in a world filled with waves of doubt, fear, depression, insecurity, and many other things holding them back. Holding them back from finding that peace and stability, which will lay out a foundation in their lives.

Many women are not achieving their dreams and goals, because they haven't first achieved that self-conscious state from within, which, after finding this, all the things they seek to do may not come at the snap of the finger, but they will come with much more ease. This ease will come from the consciousness that she "knows" her potential, her talents, and many possibilities.

So, that takes away doubt of self, because she "knows" self, takes away fear, because what is there to fear? When she "knows" if she falls in any aspect, whether physically, emotionally, mentally, spiritually, or financially, she can always get back up.

Finding the soul will replace depression with happiness and insecurity with the confidence of a queen.

I wrote this book so all women can look into it as a daily reminder that they are intelligent, beautiful, talented, ambitious, courageous, overcomers. So use it to nurture your soul, and awaken it, because many women are asleep with their eyes open. They see the world outside and around them but fail to see the power of the woman within.

Mikal Bethea

The Woman in the Ocean

    This poem is dedicated to the woman in the ocean. The ocean consists of many things that can be helpful toward success in life, or failure, things like waves, which trouble the calmness, toss you in every direction and have you choking for air. These are considered the small things that gang up and become one big problem.
    Things like relationship problems where your companion doesn't make you happy or problems raising your kids who are too grown for their age, the car needing to be fixed, loans that need to be paid etc. They come back to back constantly, and if you can't find the flow of things, they'll eventually drown you, like waves in the ocean.
    This goes out to the woman swimming towards her goals in life, gaining confidence with every stroke of her arms, and every kick of her legs. This is even for the woman just exercising her talents and sharpening her skills, or for the woman who just wants to get away. Either way, she is the woman in the ocean.

As you walk on the shore of your life, longing for times of peace./
You look ahead and behind, only to find sand as far as eyes can see./
Looking up, you're reminded of what the skies could be./
Clear, cloudy, or rainy, depending on the time of week./
This is your life, and everything consisting together./
The unknown covered by the sand that seems to be existing forever./
The sky is your mind and emotions predicting the weather./
Sometimes you are content, but wonder does it get any better./
Then something catches your eye, so you look to the right./
To find an ocean you never saw in the book of your life./
Hesitation held you back as you took it inside./
Then realized you got to jump in like a hook in a fight./
So you do, and as your feet leave sand to splash into water./
You see your life beginning to change, and snatch out of order./
You take your first stroke, knowing you can't go back to your border./

Searching For Souls

Swallow a mouthful of water, but you still push past forward./
The skies get dark, rainfalls with no umbrella to stop it./
Can't see where you're going in life, worried about whoever is watching./
That's insecurity, and a voice in your mind saying, "It's better to drop it."/
Because it will pull you down, and drowning is never an option./
So you drop it, then rain and clouds part, you've torn them away./
And realized though swimming is hard it gets easier along the way./
So you've score today, a new woman born to stay./
Keep pushing woman, you'll find another shore someday./

Mikal Bethea

In Case You Didn't Know

This poem is dedicated to those women who simply don't know; the ones who don't know who they are, which goes back to being asleep.

So you must ask the question, "If you don't know who you are, who are you acting like?" Not yourself, so, then comes the realization, if you're not living "your" life, then you're living in deception of self. And self is the worst person to deceive.

If you don't know who you are, you don't know what you want out of life, nor how to attain it. So let me tell you, in case you didn't know.

First off, your true essence is the feminine spiritual being./
The underlying source of your physical body, living and breathing./
But your true essence will only awaken when given a reason./
And bring life to the beginnings, like ending a season./
Secondly, you are a woman of importance from the beginning of birth./
A bringer of life, so now you're representing the earth./
Which feeds her people, and cries rain when witnessing hurt./
Quenching the thirst, always here listening first./
That's you, the mother of life as we watch kids grow up./
And kids are our future, taking the torch when our list rolls up./
But without you, there are no kids, there is no us./
So we need you to ride until the wheels off, and the windows bust./
So know the importance of who you are, and tend to your soul./
Queen of the earth, rise up when we're getting too low./
Believe in yourself, never say that this isn't so./
And I'm here to show, just in case you didn't know./

Perfect Imperfection

    This poem is dedicated to the woman who believes she is so imperfect. The insecure woman who always seems to focus on her faults; Too consumed in paying attention to what she does not have, to realize the power of what she does.

    If you are this woman, I encourage you to search your soul and find yourself. Because that's the only way you will find that true beauty comes from within.

All your life you never had a mind to believe in yourself./
Thinking your physical appearance is the key to your wealth./
So, when certain doors don't open, you don't understand the reason in dept./
Then break like glass, ashamed of the pieces you've kept./
And speaking of self, why don't you take time in pleasing yourself?/
No, life's not a game, but tell me why are you cheating yourself?/
Depression can lead to suicide, but that shouldn't be a reason for death./
If you hide your eyes from your prize how can you see when you step?/
You can't, so you think the place of beauty is where your friends be./
But your face isn't everything because beauty is only skin deep./
You think your imperfections are the only thing men see./
But it's the beauty of your mind and personality that real men seek./
Looking to God for an angel I told him to send me./
So you don't need to see a plastic surgeon to look like a ten piece./
He said you need a new face, but I recommend peace./
To awaken the woman inside of you who's been sleep./
Fake eyebrows and fake smiles, yeah you're dealing with those./
I like your shoes but I know they be killing your toes./
Instead of healing, these things are only killing your soul./
Taking away true beauty like peeling a rose./
So, every morning you wake up, you wake up to a lie./
Because by using makeup, you only make up a disguise./

Mikal Bethea

Don't fake surprise, I'm not saying this to be making you cry./
But make you alive, by showing you your face in the sky./
The mirror is your first enemy, you are your worst enemy that folds you in./
Baby, you're going to look the same no matter what pose you're in./
So, don't let the clothes you're in, close you in./
And when you need motivation read this and let it hold you, friend./

My Equation

I think love plays a very important role in life. Everyone needs someone. Love is the balance of life, in this case, I speak of man and woman.

A man is not complete without a woman and vice versa. But, make sure it's the man you love and be sure you understand love.

Love has many elements, many variables that sum up its solution. Like math. So I guess what I'm trying to say is that love is an equation. And this is one of my many personal poems that I will feature. I speak for every man that feels this way, to every woman that cares. This is my equation.

I want to show you my appreciation for you as a lady./
The self-importance of your true nature through my admiration./
Thinking of you makes me restless, my mind's back to pacing./
The way you walk, stride, and spark in my eyes is so fascinating./
I'm becoming infatuated in a way that I can't explain it./
You are the fire to the candle that's blazing with my impatience./
Just the sound of your voice is so amazing./
Such a sensation, killing me, got me contemplating./
On whether to take his relationship into true elevation./
Like elevators, drifting high into expectation./
Don't let others fake you, your self-worth is far greater./
When they treat you like trash, I look at you as high maintenance./
To be in your presence is truly a blessing, be my acquaintance./
I'll be romantic and our relations to heighten up my persuasion./
I want to adorn you, praise you like my creator./
My earth, wrap my arms around you like the equator./
Life with you is like wine, I'm savoring each flavor./
And you are my sight, doing my eyes a deep favor./
Hypnotized by the smell of your body, a sweet fragrance./
Have you ever smelled something so strong that you could taste it?/
That's you, my earth Angel./
The breath of my life, the solution to my equation./
I want to show you love through my utmost dedication./
My foundation, let me open your eyes to a revelation./

Mikal Bethea

That you should be catered to every day, not just on occasions./
No masquerading, except lovemaking when the mask is on my face./
And, if me plus you kissing equals me dying in this equation./
Then I must say, the taste of death has a serious temptation./
But let me die in your arms of your embrace./
Through meditation, I'll see life through your eyes, in my equation./

The Mirror of Love

    This is one of my personal poems. It deals with the inspection of your significant other. To see if they coincide with what you want out of life. If they don't, then they are contradicting to your goals, and therefore, holding you back.

    When two people love each other, they become mirror reflections of one another. And when combined, they make up the mirror of love.

Do you ever look inside yourself for a clearer perception./
Of the things you want the most, but you fear the expression?/
The emotion that guards your heart with simple protection./
Hard to test it, stressing, because all you're hearing is questions./
But when you look inside, do you see it as a picture selection?/
With imperfections? Because love is like a mirror reflection./
And your heart has been scarred from years of deception./
So you take nothing on face value because your feelings will test it./
I've got to respect it because everything needs inspection./
But love is a thief; it takes you when you least expect it./
I can feel your heart, and I hear that you're desperate./
Every time I lean close and put my ear in your section./
I ask, "Can you feel my love?" Are you hearing the message?/
If so, don't hold back, or fear the connection./
Just fill like refreshments as I fill you with blessings./
Have you swimming in presents and never hear a rejection./
The only woman that can make me shed a tear in her presence./
That's you, my angel to bring me clearer and nearer to heaven./
Your mind is food for my soul; let me eat you for breakfast./
Leaving my mark, hoping that you see the impression./
Because the love I have for you is above an obsession./
So every time you look into this mirror, feel my love and affection./

Mikal Bethea

Mental Sex

    This poem coincides with the mirror of love. But it deals with putting moral priorities first. Many women will have sex with a man before getting to know that man. Sex will bring forth strong emotions. Strong emotion will blind you, to the point you can't tell the difference between love and lust.
    Therefore, the sex that needs to be done is mental. Sex is the joining of two bodies. So, the joining of two minds is mental sex.

Let me take a peek into your mind with the best of my ability./
While most men want to sex you physically, let me make love to you mentally./
I'll keep on digging, knowing I'll find you eventually./
As I go deeper than history, so you'll always remember me./
Seeing you tortured and suffering from poor judgment is killing me./
When you should be smiling, asking, "Why do all the angels envy me?"/
It's best to be friends before lovers to make you my centerpiece./
Building a foundation for our relation so nothing can intervene./
To intertwine both minds so spiritually./
And at the same time, filling you with that much more of intimacy./
Dedicating my life to making you happy like a religious belief./
Just believe and I'll make your spirit catch your soul making you scream./
I want to be the voice in the back of your mind making you think./
That you're a queen, and that's why when men look at you, they don't blink./
So, when you think of me, you'll say, "He's so much of a friend to me."/
And if this is wrong, I guess I'm the government's worst enemy./
Prepared to face the consequences of my iniquities./
If this is truly an iniquity then I guess I'm a filthy beast./
S-E-X, most men want to do it physically./
But to make sure it was meant to be, let's make love mentally./

I'm Still... You're Still... We're Still...

Dealing with relationships is a full-time job between both partners. Troubles and many problems come and go, but you must always keep in mind who you are. That's who you are as individuals and who you are together.

So, with that said, when problems arise stick it out and work it out. And at the end of the day, be able to tell each other I'm still, you're still, we're still...

I don't know about you, but I contemplate on what the future will hold./
The expectations of my desires on this beautiful road./
Yeah, I hide my feelings until I choose to be known./
But you see right through me, tell me what you truly behold./
They say a heart is a house for love; is mine your home?/
Many men want to give you their lives, but it's mine you own./
It takes more than glasses to read, more than a mind to know./
And more than hands to feel, what love does to the soul./
But I'm still... You're still... We're still.../
Here, so I assume the love is real./
You are the light of my life, the reason I love to live./
Your smile brings the reassurance that a hug will give./
And even though life empties the cup that only love can fill./
I'm still... You're still... We're still.../
In love, and even a bomb couldn't blow it apart./
I want to show you how happiness can make you glow in the dark./
That blind people could say they know who you are./
And even though you call me a thief because I stole your heart./
I'm still... You're still... We're still.../
Able to grow, still able to go./
I want to teach you things about love you weren't able to know./
To plant seeds in your life you weren't able to sow./
And bring angels to your feet like we're playing in snow./
I'm still... You're still... We're still...
Bound tight, yeah, that sounds right./
I was dead, but since I've found you, I've found life./
Me without you, now tell me what does that sound like?/

Mikal Bethea

That sounds like sun without light, or, stars without night./
So, I'm still... You're still... We're still...
Everything, refuse to let go, we can't run./
Selfish over our love like cake, others can taste none./
Afraid of the death that will take this fun./
But nevertheless, until that day comes./
I'm still... You're still... We're still…

The Real You

They say hell has no fury like that of a woman scorned. That's sad. And it pains my heart to see a woman walk around mad at the world. Life is short; too short to be lived with hatred dwelling in the heart.

If you are this woman, I hope and pray you wake up tomorrow and realize it's not worth it. Harboring these emotions will literally change you. And the person you were will cease to exist. And this new disguise will hide the real you.

Let me start by asking, why do you let them conceal you?/
And by "them" I mean the men of your past who've made you so stereotypical./
And miserable, it's visual even through my peripheral./
That the person you are portraying to be is not the real you./
Our most brilliant lies are those we reserve for ourselves to kill the truth./
You bring others into deception, but how can you deceive the real you?/
The one who likes to smile and joke with individuals./
You have allowed others to push you into a nutshell with so much ridicule./
You need a real man to show you upliftment is critical./
To breakup your hard front showing you what a kiss can do./
To melt the foundation of the person standing in the midst of you./
Longing for someone to cherish her grabbing the moment by the fistful./
Let's be grown, and stop playing games like kids do./
Because this impersonation you are putting in place just doesn't fit you./
Let me bring you to the realization that this is proof./
Your true characteristics are priceless, you shouldn't live by a list of rules./
The real you comes out of hiding so I can get a clear view./
To show you there are some men in this world who are still true./
You have been hiding so long, you probably wonder is the sky still blue?/

Mikal Bethea

It is too, but angels look at your disguise like it's pitiful./
When your smile would open heaven and make it shine like crystals do./
More precious than cars and clothes to a rich fool./
And you could be enriched too./
If you would just be, the real you./

Searching For Souls

Dreaming

    This is the last of my more personal poems dealing with love and relationships. This one is dedicated to women who felt like they didn't or don't have an effect on men's lives.
    Most people believe females are the ones hurt the most during breakups. That's not always the case. Sometimes it's the male, but his pride won't allow him to show it.
    Many women don't realize how much of an impact they have. Well, I'm here to speak for any and every man you left dreaming.

Everyone dreams of things that they may perceive./
Are only make-believe, by the way they seem./
Plenty nights I've played scenes of you as I lay asleep./
Of you having my baby, loving me so faithfully./
If we wouldn't have separated I wonder how things would be./
But I can't change the past and that's pure pain to me./
So I dream... Hoping that whenever you think of me./
It brings a smile to your face as big as maple trees./
The dreams are so real I know it wasn't fake love./
And the worst part comes at the time I wake up./
My heart races and beats in my chest like a great rush./
Feeling your soul enter mine right after we break touch./
I cherish these dreams like pure gold; reality I can't touch./
Always hearing your voice in the back of my mind I can't hush./
So I dream... Of things I physically can't touch./
Creating pictures with my mind, using my emotions as my paintbrush./
I only sleep through half the night; reality has a price./
Taking me away from dreams, but for you, I have to fight./
I'd give up half my life to hear you laugh tonight./
Because you fill a gap in my life, the only patch of my life./
I now realize I connected a trap to my light./
And there's no greater feeling on earth than to have a wife./
So I dream... With more emotion than the passion of Christ./
I'd die just for you to have a happier life./
I hope my emotions are like messages to you./
When words can't explain how I show reverence to you./

Mikal Bethea

Dreaming of times I bought presents just for you./
I'd wake up and swear I smell your presence in my room./
Treat you like a goddess, to do whatever you shall choose./
Going crazy for your love, so is there a heaven for a fool?/
So I dream... Of many things that keep my head under the blues./
And until we reunite, I'm preparing for you./

The Rose Growing by the Cliff

    I dedicate this poem to the woman who is symbolic to the rose. Roses are beautiful, their fragrances are sweet, their petals as soft as velvet.

    They say the most beautiful roses are found in the hardest places to reach, like a cliff. But you must be careful of how to pick these roses because they've been through some things. As a result, then towards the edge is where they lean. Their thorns are sharper, longer than average. They have grown in solitude, ignored by the rest of the world. Known, yet unknown as the rose growing by the cliff.

Beautiful you are in your colors of glory./
Alone on this cliff, time ticks as you further your story./
Stuck to the earth, it hurts to see others are soaring./
While you're leaning, looking down as the waters are roaring./
No one there to keep you dry as the rain is pouring./
So you pray and pray, for the sun to come bring the morning./
Holding on the faith when it seems everything else is moisty./
Happy with what you get, you know beggars can't be choosey./
Trying to square time away, but you are facing a round hour./
Living in solitude so people call you a crowd coward./
They don't understand you, so they call you a wildflower./
Your expressions are your voice, so all you do is smile louder./
Even when you feel like you're falling, you laugh with strange delight./
You don't change your site because you're not afraid of heights./
Friends with the moon, so you're not afraid of nights./
Your whole life's been a battle, yet you continue to face the fight./
You shine bright like candles do; men want to sample you./
Beauty and strength, they got to be careful how they handle you./
Many have tried, failed, and learned it's a gamble too./
Ended up slipping off the cliff, they stumbled and trampled too./
And you watched as they fell below, flowing by the drift./
Their last seconds spent reaching for beauty, glowing like a gift./
So close, but he missed, but only by a slip./
Just another man trying to grab the rose growing by the cliff./

Mikal Bethea

The Single Parent-Mother

This poem is dedicated to the single parent-mother. I'm always passionate when dealing with this subject because I've witnessed it firsthand.

My mother, who is the definition of a survivor, raised her three kids alone. Our fathers were in prison, leaving her by herself. I saw the things my mother had difficulty handling, from the result of raising three kids. And they range from physical exhaustion due to her working long hours. Emotional stress from the pressure of not knowing where the next meal would come from, etcetera.

She was so focused on providing for her kids, she had no time to focus on herself. Determined not to let them go through what she went through, she didn't take the time to search her soul. Too occupied, just a result of being the single parent-mother.

I understand the pressures you feel running like a race in your bones./
The struggles of life you fight and have to face on your own./
Never thought being a mother would take so much when patience is gone./
You take it and groan because you've got kids to raise on your own./
Work, work, and provide; laziness has no place in your home./
And most men don't want women with kids, so relations are gone./
Son gets older, now he's got the nerve to be thinking he's grown./
Discipline him time after time hoping he's not taking it wrong./
Because you know he's confused with no father around./
Can't pretend or say this doesn't bother the house./
No food in the house will really bother the mouth./
Because stomach pains will even bother a mouse./
At birth, it was diapers and baby milk, hugs to baby them./
Baby dolls and spaceships, when no one would play with them./
But to a boy, it's okay with you because life is a stadium./
But as he gets older, you lose the words to say to him./
Don't know how to raise a man when you haven't raised yourself./
Baby's father picked up and left when he should've stayed and helped./

Searching For Souls

You crave for balance in your home more than you prayed for wealth./
And it's sad when the dad's incarcerated in jail./
As a single parent-mother, life can be like days in a hell./
But, don't let your emotions be keys to lock you away in a cell./
Instead, sit back and take time to breathe./
Clear the vision of the thoughts and take time to see./
And find yourself; don't let your soul play hide and seek./
Meditate at different times of the week to put your mind at ease./
Because that's the only way to find the peace./
The same peace that will carry you when you're tired and weak./
But, it starts with you, the foundation, bread, and butter./
Stand, don't shudder, make it said, don't stutter./
Mold your life, don't let it be shaped by the hands of another./
And show the world it's possible to make it being the single parent-mother./

Mikal Bethea

She's a Brick House

I dedicate this poem to the woman built like a brick house. There are many who are "physically" built like a brick house, but the one I speak of is mental.

This is for the strong woman, the confident, overcomer. She who has searched herself, been through hardships in life, and yet still, she's a brick house.

Men worship your presence when they can't get to you./
Beauty in the form of intelligence, you're known to trick a few./
Or maybe they tricked themselves thinking they could hit and move./
Everyone makes choices, but you make it hard to pick and choose./
Between a million women, none can say they're built like you./
Foundation built from the confidence you fill like shoes./
Your surroundings could crumble and open like a fist might do./
But you stick like glue while other women slip right through./
I guess the obstacles you face are only steps to your porch./
To be stomped on repeatedly before others step to your door./
To twist the knob of your heart as we step to your core./
Where the fire is so hot you might melt to the floor./
That's your ambition, something not too many others are given./
Or in others, it's hidden, but you mother your wishes./
And raise them up in life to another position./
A roof to cover your rooms, but that could never cover your limits./
Birds and planes could never reach the place of your dreams./
The queen of life, the earth is yours, you take as you please./
Take it and leave it, it's amazing how you take it with ease./
If money were leaves, I could see you shaking a tree./
You weren't born like this or built from a lot of sticks./
It took risk on top of risk, to be laid down brick on top of brick./
You've survived hail, sleet, and snow, and wore them like clothes that got to fit./
Wind blow, but you say to yourself, *"Ain't nothing stopping this!"*/
She's a brick house, beautiful walls and big couch./

Searching For Souls

She's a brick house, don't pay the lease, get kicked out./
If you've never seen one in your life you've missed out./
Never for sale, but the sign in the yard said, "She's a brick house!"/

Mikal Bethea

The Mirror of Life

    This poem is dedicated to the woman in the mirror. The woman staring at her reflection and breaking herself down.
    Looking into the mirror is very similar to looking inside you. Because, when looking at your reflection, your mind is telling you what you think about what you're seeing. What you think about what you're seeing will help determine your success in life.
    Because, if what you see, is what you "think" is a failure, that's what you'll be. But if what you see, is what you "think" is a queen, then that you will manifest.

So, what do you think of yourself when you look into the mirror of life?/
How many times have you found yourself staring at the mirror of life?/
Money can't buy happiness, but you still try to figure the price./
Are you looking at your physical, or what's bigger for life?/
Are you the bringer of darkness, or the giver of light?/
Pick through the layers of your doubt like a digger for life./
Because doubting yourself will melt your validation like a pillar of ice./
Fear will water you down like liquor with ice./
But don't go blind, think positive and trigger your sight./
So you can see the mirror clearly, without fractions without asking./
And realize what you're packing, not what you're lacking./
Because your thoughts are ropes to bring back what you're attracting./
Self-image is like an act but you're not acting./
Because what you see will be the exact without subtracting./
And your success will only come when you're reacting./
Nothing will just fall in your lap while you are relaxing./
Put forth effort and go take what you're asking./
See pain's a small thing, but they differ in height./
When obstacles come, be slow to retreat, but quicker to fight./
Search the woman in the mirror until the picture is bright./
Until you feel like the picture is right./

Searching For Souls

Keep the fire in your eyes in this river of ice./
Because even at night there's a flicker of light./
I know the taste of living can be bitter or nice./
But think of yourself as an overcomer in this mirror of life./

Mikal Bethea

Broken Promises

This poem is dedicated to the woman who has been sold dreams all her life. People abandoned her when they promised to always be there. Some sold her dreams of life being easy-going, no pain, or struggles. But, life turned out to be an uphill battle.

Men in her life lied, cheated, and treated her like nothing when they promised to be loyal, committed, and dedicated to catering to her.

So, now she has trust issues. She stereotypes men as being dogs, because of the ones in her past. Slow to accept friendship, because when she needed one the most, they were nowhere to be found. All of this is a result of the many broken promises.

It started from childhood, when people said things to sound good./
Like Santa will bring you presents if you behave like a child should./
As time passed, you gained common sense like any child would./
Then your dreams burned to ashes like fire around wood./
Some promised to be friends until the end, and friends are tightly bound./
But they are nowhere to be found as you fight for the crown./
All alone in the dark in a night with no sound./
No one hears your cries, but there's a million people right in the town./
This is money, so you cut corners as time dies./
People painted you dreams, but a beautiful picture means nothing to blind eyes./
I'm searching for souls; I know you're thinking, *"I hope that he finds me."*/
But I'm only a helper; it's up to you to catch your soul when it flies by./
Men promise you the universe just to break your stars apart./
Knocked your lights out, now your stars are dark./
Made you feel less of a woman, and your fire hard to spark./
Played with your mind, twisted your emotions, and scarred your heart./
Left you with kids to raise, trying to fix a broken home./

Searching For Souls

Wondering can broke promises heal like broken bones?/
Take action, and let it be your soul you focus on./
And turn your life into sweet melodies and not broken songs./
Encourage yourself, keep hope, and a lot of it./
Your treasure is on the inside, hold tight, don't drop a cent./
Leave everyone who lied, stuck in unspoken astonishment.
And put the pieces of your life back together that shattered from broken promises./

Mikal Bethea

Acceptance of Self

I dedicate this poem to the woman having a hard time accepting herself, the woman going through the emotion of self-hate.

As people, we all seek acceptance, even in adulthood. I've dealt with, and spoken to a lot of women who simply can't accept themselves. Some get plastic surgery to change this, or liposuction to change that, not realizing the thing that needed changing was where the hands can't feel and the eyes can't see. That's from within.

It takes more than a scalpel to cut away the feeling of self-hate. And mascara could never cover the pain that comes with it.

Some women just don't love themselves and strive to change into what others think is right, all for acceptance. But, I'm here to tell you that you must first have acceptance of self.

Many women are picking life up from the place it was shook./
Looking for comfort and acceptance in the face of a crook./
Just waiting to be swallowed like bait on a hook./
Questioning everything, from their personality, to the way that they look./
On an emotional roller coaster, thoughts race like mice on a semi-course./
To gain control of these thoughts, it takes time and plenty force./
Being ashamed of who you are will leave you subjected to any voice./
Mental abuse will make you accept attention from any source./
That's the reason why in relationships, men run over you./
To the point family and friends don't notice you./
Give him money for simple things, when your rents overdue./
And every time they leave in the end you're so confused./
Let me show you how to guard yourself, and defend like soldiers do./
And build a foundation that won't be moved by multitudes./
First off, be who you are; there is no need to make self-tacky./
Focus on your own life; stop trying to make everyone else happy./
Because they'll treat you like trash; have you ever felt classy?/

Searching For Souls

Even walking barefoot through fire you must step gladly./
Because things will only get better when you are yourself./
I can search your soul, but it's up to you to accept./
When there is nothing left to hold onto, hold onto yourself./
When there's nothing left to belong to, then belong to yourself./
Being rich in the things that wealth just can't bring./
Fix what you can, and learn to accept what you can't change./
Health and happiness should dwell on the same chain./
If you don't allow your thoughts to get cloudy well, it can't rain./
So learn to love who you are, and your preference felt./
Don't shape your life to fit others; that's deception of self./
Mental suicide is a perception of death./
But you can begin a new life through acceptance of self./

Mikal Bethea

<u>Faith in Self</u>

This poem is dedicated to the woman who doesn't have a lot of faith in self, which could be the result of many things, from childhood experiences, to being downgraded to the point of having no self-worth, or from just being in an environment where it seems like everyone is helpless or it may come from low self-esteem.

If you're this woman, I want you to know faith is the first key to the many doors of success. This is the factor of happiness, confidence, and motivation to reach higher.

Faith lies on the inside, where it is nurtured to grow. You must be able to see yourself achieving in order to achieve. Then believe, and have faith in self.

Some women lack faith but are praying to God to reveal./
A revelation, waiting for inspiration they would probably feel./
If they would have patience and let faith show how they feel./
If you don't think you can succeed, then nobody will./
And if they do, it won't matter; it's up to you to go after./
If you don't, then it's the truth you won't capture./
Have faith, and work off it; if you lose, then don't shatter./
Get back up and climb, but don't choose the wrong ladder./
Don't pay attention to heights and negative things others say./
Sticks and stones break bones, but words can't hurt a face./
Trials and tribulations should be used to face another day./
I guess that's where your cover lays, so never turn another way./
Tell yourself you're going to make it until you believe it./
Set out a goal, and don't stop reaching until you achieve it./
Put your roots in the soil of faith, and refuse to leave it./
The taller your trees get, the more beautiful your leaves get./
You must picture yourself at the finish line when your vision is out./
Open your ears to motivation and don't listen to doubt./
You should go out and grab what you're wishing about./
Chasing your dreams in life, now that's what livings about./
They say the sky's the limit, but that's not true./
How's the sky the limit, when man walked on the moon?/
So have faith as you walk in your shoes, you're walking to prove./

Searching For Souls

There's nothing you can't do when you've been through what you've been through./
Even if life shuffles the cards but you don't like the way they're dealt./
Never allow it to change the way you step./
Don't focus on the many days filled with pain you've felt./
Just believe, and know you'll make it if you have faith in self./

Mikal Bethea

Keep Keeping Your Head Up

Life is filled with struggles, some big some small. But, you must learn to use these struggles as tools of motivation. Gain the willpower to free yourself from your unfortunate circumstances.

Through it all, remain focused, remain firm on your foundation, and remain confident. No matter what happens, never let your obstacles see you sweat. Yes, times get hard, but don't get soft.

Fight fire with fire or even with water if you have to. The harder life pushes you, the harder you push back. When it feels like you can't go any further, that's when you go the hardest. Things will get better as long as you fight the good fight. As long as there is breath in your lungs, keep keeping your head up.

Life's filled with storms, but sometimes you must embrace the rain./
I know it hurts, but you have to face the pain./
Because sometimes that's what it takes to gain./
When life tries to hold you down you must break the chain./
The struggles are here, there's really no name to blame./
So be known as a success while others chase for fame./
When life fights with fire then create the same./
If you get knocked off the tracks, then chase the train./
And keep keeping your head up... Don't lose sense of reality./
Keep on battling with everything that's happening./
Understand that things can change dramatically./
From good to bad, bad to good, or success to tragedy./
When the game gets hard you must adventure strategy./
Go through to get through; you can't always live lavishly./
Some obstacles can destroy what you made a masterpiece./
And even though you ask, "Is this the way it has to be?"/
Keep keeping your head up... And build from the basics./
Speak motivation to self even when it's difficult to say./
Believe you'll make it, even when it's impossible to explain it./
In any circumstance or situation./
Keep keeping your head up... Stay focused and pay attention./
No matter your position, keep flowing with your intentions./

Searching For Souls

Voices in your mind will speak, so just listen./
Because, that's your strongest tool, a woman's intuition./
So keep keeping your head up... Even when the time is stalling./
Cries are calling, and the devil in disguise is clawing./
When the picture in your mind is foggy./
When your eyes are foggy, even when the sky is falling./
Keep keeping your head up.../

Mikal Bethea

One In A Million

    I was once in a relationship with a beautiful female. I won't call her name. But, one day over the phone, she called herself pretty. She considered herself as being like any other female.
    So, I told her, "I think you're beautiful."
    She paused for a second and replied, "No one has ever told me that before."
    Then I asked, "No one, not even you?"
    "No." she replied.
    This really amazed me, because she "really" was beautiful but didn't believe it. She thought, from her overall standpoint, she was like any other woman. But, I don't believe any two women are the same. Each one is one in a million.

If you stood in a crowd, would you stand out?/
When they call for beautiful women, would you step forward or stand down?/
If I say you were a queen, would you understand how?/
You could walk into a building and make every man bow./
But you don't realize this because you're tied to the act./
I can see your eyes are open, but you're blind to the fact./
You think you are ordinary; that's a lie to be exact./
The same thing that binds your soul, it's probably a trap./
Who's the crook then? Don't play the role of the fool./
Because that's just a tool to keep you so confused./
With the underestimation of the things you could do./
And have you blind to investigate the things you can't prove./
You should shine like the light illuminating from the moon./
Showing reflections of your mind like a dime in a pool./
You are one in a million in this mirror vision./
But your attention is not in it, you're looking for wishes./
Someone said you were amazing, but you wouldn't listen./
So you feel like a woman who is crazy with no intuition./
Too busy looking where your faults are at./
You think you are like any other woman; you're not a copycat./
Your life has too many actions for you to not react./

Searching For Souls

You share "some" qualities with others, but you're still an individual./
No two women are the same, not even in the physical./
But you won't understand until you search your spiritual./
And bring the realization into your mental./
You're one in a million./

Ms. Independent

There's nothing more attractive than an independent woman; A conscious woman with the purpose of life. She knows what she wants out of life, and puts forth her all to attain it.

She doesn't rely on anyone but herself. She never has her hand out just waiting for something to be given to her. She has searched herself and found inner peace, which causes her outer self to blossom and bloom like flowers.

She doesn't live her life in depression, nor in the shackles of insecurity, stress, self-hate, ignorance, or any other form of chaos that leaves one mentally dead.

She is aware of what's going on around her and is able and willing to change anything wrong. She has morals, goals, and standards she lives by, and the mind state that nothing can stop her but her.

If you are this woman, I dedicate this poem to you. If you're not, I pray this poem encourages you to elevate your mind, body, and soul. Because that's what it takes to become Ms. Independent.

This goes out to Ms. Independent, you know who you are./
No one on earth has to show you that you are./
The hardships of life could never throw you too far./
Shining bright, but we still promote you a star./
Beautiful mind, and a beautiful soul too./
You control life, you don't allow it to control you./
Only you can hold you the way a person is supposed to./
But men still worship the ground you walk on when your body strolls through./
Sophisticated with inspiration, you stay motivated./
To the point it's amazing, anything you want you can take it./
Confidence is your perfume, every morning you spray it./
Now it seems like every woman is wanting your fragrance./
Little girls see your success, and looking up to you too./
As you stomp on doubt like gum stuck to your shoes./
You know and understand, even the toughest can lose./
But falling is really nothing to you./
You just get back up and forget that stuff./

Searching For Souls

Failure and success? You could never mix that up./
Your life was broken; you decided to fix that up./
Your soul was sleep; you went searching to pick that up./
Saw what you wanted in life and became relentless./
Now people who said you'd fall beg for forgiveness./
You're in a competition with no one worthy to contend with./
So today we applaud you, and crown you as Ms. Independent./

Mikal Bethea

You Deserve

I dedicate this poem to women, period. All women deserve. They deserve to be appreciated, catered to, and put on a pedestal. They deserve to be able to feel good about themselves, to have the finer things in life. Women deserve to be respected because they are important.

They deserve all of this just because they are who they are, women. God's greatest gift to man wasn't a dog, it wasn't riches, it was the woman.

They say, "Men run the world." Well, I say, "Men run the world that women cradled in their arms."

Besides every great man, there was a strong woman. She was his backbone, his support, or maybe even the one running the show in the background. She was his mirror image, his counterpart that made him complete.

Women don't sit below men to be trampled on. If anything, they should be right beside them to catch them from falling to the wayside. Because we men can sometimes be stupid and selfish, but always remember, you deserve.

Every woman in the world deserves special attention./
With no ulterior motives ever intended./
Forever exquisite, though she would never admit it./
We love your touch, whether it's hugs or whether it's kisses./
You give us purpose, and life to the living person./
Though the world can be a circus, just know that you still deserve it./
Blessings to kill the curses, to show that you're still perfect./
Even at times when you're down, you should still feel worth it./
Never worthless, our foundation beneath the surface./
With no curtains, you deserve it, even if you never heard it./
The world is yours. You're our queen, were only servants./
To cater to you and propose our every service./
You deserve to stride when you walk, speak with pride when you talk./
Visualize what you want with the eyes of a hawk./
With the power to effect all the lives that saw./

Searching For Souls

You're the truth we use to erase lives like chalk./
You deserved a list of rigid of diamonds and pearls./
A nameplate that says, "The finest of girls,"/
To sit back while the fingers of happiness are intertwining your curls./
You are the knot that we tied to the world./

Mikal Bethea

<u>Love is Blind</u>

They say love is blind, and anything that goes blind starts to deal with the sense of feeling. It touches, it probes, it pokes, and it rubs until it feels safe to take another step forward. But, just because the steps was safe, that doesn't necessarily mean the environment you stepped in is.

This goes to show that, just as your eyes can be deceiving, so can your feelings and your emotions. So, if love is an emotion, then yes, love can be blind.

But it also depends on the person it's coming from. If that person is blind, with no understanding of love, then they will call any feeling that brings pleasure, "love."

But to a woman who's conscious of self and love, she'll compare what she wants out of a relationship with what she has. She will compare her feelings with logical thinking to see if things add up correctly. She will touch, probe, poke, and rub for the right place to put her heart, because she knows, love is blind.

Every time you fall, you chase your redemption./
Scramble in codes, you try to arrange decryption./
Hard to picture, so you strive to change description./
Sometimes sickening, and love is the only prescription./
But love is blind; sometimes it can drug the mind./
To make you wonder why do you put up with lies./
You try to hug your pride, but can't ignore the tug inside./
Sometimes, you've got to rub your eyes, because love is blind./
So it deals with feeling, and feeling deals with emotions./
He's done you so wrong, yet you give him devotion./
Love is an ocean, and you constantly move with the motion./
Under a spell, you know it, but refuse the potion./
You tolerate a lot of things, you wouldn't dare to react./
He comes home late with no explanation of where he was at./
You're playing your role, more confused with every act./
When it comes to the relationship, you're the one carrying that./
Love is blind, and it can be masked like Halloween./
The book of a lot of dreams, if you know how to read./

Searching For Souls

If not, it'll leave you with a whole lot of pleas./
Confused to the point you don't know how to leave./
That's when you need to go inside, expose the lies,/
And hang them out like clothes to dry./
To be sure the two of you are compatible and all points arise./
To make you realize love isn't born to die./
But still, love is blind./

Mikal Bethea

Just Breathe

Sometimes the obstacles in life can seem like giants, like, no matter what you do, they still keep coming. To the point, you feel helpless, so small, so vulnerable, and nothing will work. Your mind is racing, and you can't accomplish anything because you can't focus on one thing. The job is not paying enough, bills on top of bill's, relationship falling, health problems, and problems in the family. If it's not one thing, it's another.

But remember, the less you think of yourself, the stronger these things become. You can't run from them because they'll just keep building up. So you must fight the good fight.

You have to get your thoughts in order, then your problems too. Sort them out, big from small. Solve the small ones to gain strength and confidence to face the bigger ones.

Find a place of solitude, where you can be alone with nothing and no one bothering you. Think, don't panic, don't get stressed out, because they can lead to a mental breakdown. When things are coming at a constant rate, close your eyes, relax, and just breathe.

It's hard to keep your mind straight when life makes you want to curl in./
And it feels like your thoughts are stuck in a world wind./
The mind is like a treasure box, where riches should twirl in./
So don't put trash inside the box that you keep your pearls in./
You look in the mirror; it seems like you're facing a stranger./
Frustrated with situations, persuading your anger./
But stare into the eyes of the beast as you're facing the danger./
And stay connected to your soul, like interlacing your fingers./
Though you go through a storm, you must still remain./
Strong, even though it seems like nobody feels your pain./
Your soul is fire, don't let anything kill the flame./
Praying for a thief in the night to steal your rain./
From a low-paying job, with bills flying sky high./
Looking for relations, but you can't find the right guy./
Losing vision of purpose in your left and your right eye./
When desperation sets in and emotions flyby./
But change with your desire, there is no taming a lion./

Searching For Souls

Fight hard until you retire, the fire without a lighter./
Grip life without pliers, the lyrics without a writer./
Be quicker than any tiger, with more heart than a firefighter./
Believe in yourself, never let trust leave./
Be addicted to ambition like drugs when the rush leaves./
You're the tree of life and we just want to touch leaves./
So when problems come your way, stay calm, and just breathe./

Mikal Bethea

You Already Are

There was once this peaceful and United African tribe whose chief had died. When he died, so did the peace, so did the unity.

People started stealing from each other. Fights broke out, and some led to deaths. Without a chief, there was no law.

So, one day, a man named Hotep said, "I will become chief and bring peace and unity back to my tribe."

To become chief, one had to climb the highest mountain and grab an eagle's egg from the nest, then bring the egg back down without the slightest crack.

Hotep climbed the mountain, slipped a couple of times, and almost died in the process. He went through cold nights and rainy days thinking of nothing but his mission as winds tried to knock him down. But he got the egg, brought it back to the tribe, became chief, and brought peace and unity back to the tribe.

Inside his tent, he told himself, *"I've been through too much to just throw this egg away."* So he put the egg inside the chicken pen. The baby eagle hatched some time later and was raised amongst the chickens. She adapted the ways of a chicken and never learned to fly, thinking she was a chicken.

One day as the baby eagle was outside, she saw a bird in the sky, calling out. She asked the mother chicken, "What kind of bird is that?"

The mother chicken said, "That's an eagle, one of the most beautiful, majestic birds alive."

Then the baby eagle replied, "Wow! When I grow up, I want to be just like an eagle!" Two weeks later, the baby eagle died.

The baby eagle died wanting to be something she already was. She was already an eagle. She was born with the ability to fly. And this is how a lot of women are.

They died wanting to be beautiful, wanting to be "someone," wanting to be special. Well, open your eyes if you are this woman, and realize you already are.

No matter what others think as this life leaps on./
It'll be your judgment or self that your mind leans on./

Searching For Souls

Some women murder self-worth; that's where the crime scene's on./
Though they are beautiful, everything in their mind seems wrong./
So, the mind becomes the field where lies be sown./
When it should remain pure, that's not where lies belong./
Just try to be strong when the climb seems long./
As the minutes tick away and the time seems long./
I don't understand how you could think of yourself and downgrade./
That's like putting shackles and chains around slaves./
To hear a woman speak less of herself just sounds strange./
And she'll fall with shame whenever the ground caves./
You already are the things that leave us so energized./
Food for the soul we need to eat like dinnertime./
The way you think of you should look right in a sinner's eyes./
Shed away problems like trees do leaves in the wintertime./
You should be able to look into a mirror without crying./
And say, "I love myself," every time without lying./
Search your soul until you find what's been hiding./
Pursue it with such passion you will shine without trying./
The path to peace is narrow, don't take a crooked bend./
Doing nothing as the pressure of life keep pushing in./
This will be the truth no matter who's book it's in./
That your soul's a home, don't be on the outside looking in./
So you want to shine like the heavenly star?/
Or to be able to heal the sick with seventy scars?/
Or to be considered a queen wherever you are?/
That's like wanting to be a woman you already are./

The World is yours

The world is yours, and everything in it. If you want the riches, cars, clothes, and fame, you can have it. If you want the peace, you can have that too.

Everyone dreams, some dream big, some dream small. But very few people will chase those dreams. Instead, they become content with lower things that the world consists of, like poverty, depression, oppression, confusion, chaos, failure, etc.

My question is, "Why, why accept 'these' things when the whole world is yours? Why let things rule and control your life when you have the power to destroy them?" I guess it's easier to slowly drift down into the murky waters of life's sorrows. Be careful, because some have been known to drown in these same waters.

I dedicate this poem to the woman slowly falling with no motivation. Let me help you up, to show you, the world is yours.

Is the way you view life as big as it will ever get?/
Do you believe you can have the whole world as your settlement?/
All you have to do is never quit and settle this./
Get inside your elements and exercise intelligence./
This is so evident, you don't even need evidence./
Of the power you represent to make failure irrelevant./
The world is yours, but there're too many places you've never been./
You're rich beyond imagination with the money you never spend./
You don't have to be asleep to chase your dreams in life./
You can achieve things you've never dreamed in life./
So reach and turn your nightmare into a dream of life./
Then wake up and bring your dreams to life./
A lot of people will say that everything brings a price./
But you could pay it and have everything in sight./
So build over your fear and all things that lead to fright./
Believe and fight; overcome to seize the night./
I want to search your soul to the point you're feeling me./
Enough to let "you" take over your life so willingly./
It's up to you to have faith in your abilities./

Searching For Souls

And grasp everything in your ability./
Just to make your soul glow, and to let your soul know./
The many ways you can change to help your soul grow./
To be able to see clearly, even when the snow blows./
Because you hold the world in the palm of your hand like a snow globe./
The world is yours./

Mikal Bethea

Superwoman

    I think this is another one that speaks for itself, a dedication to the great women the world's been blessed to have: the daughters who took care of their parents in old age, the passionate caring mothers devoted to the well-being of their children, the loyal wives committed to stand by their husbands through thick and thin no matter what.
    The strong, graceful, and wise grandmothers, you have blessed generations with the knowledge to elevate; the amazing aunts who stepped to the plate to give understanding in times of confusion.
    Last but certainly not least, the sisters, aggravating during youth, but the shoulder we lean on as time passes and life gets hard.
    We show reverence to you all. Where would we be without you? The love and guidance you give us are truly priceless. Though at times we take you for granted, just know, you are appreciated, our breath of life, our most precious jewel, our hero, superwoman.

    You're our angels without wings who dropped down to save us./
    When times were dangerous, and the change of life would slave us./
    When we were emotionally broke, it was your love that paid us./
    The supernatural strength you used during labor that made us./
    It took that same supernatural strength to raise us./
    To the people we are today. It's strange but,/
    It's true; it was you who we gave trust./
    To hold onto when irrelevant things would shake us./
    Trials and tribulations came and were only another test to you./
    You broke them down to pieces until they were just a few./
    Superwoman flying over obstacles, they can get the best of you./

Searching For Souls

The type of attitude that makes the devil mad at you./
Because you overcame, completing all that you had to do./
All the money in the world couldn't amount to half of you./
We don't even have to choose; you are our absolute./
But you don't need compliments to satisfy your confidence./
You know your importance of self through spiritual consciousness./
You are a queen. We can see you are; it's common sense./
We stand in awe as you continue to shine with your accomplishments./
So, when we needed love and affection, you were the woman./
When we were stuck in depression, you were the woman./
When we were looking for mother's, you were the woman./
When we needed knocks across the head, you were the woman./
Superwoman./

Mikal Bethea

M.O.B

I believe every woman should have her M.O.B. It will bring understanding to her being, and clarity to her vision. She will not be swayed by emotions because she'll think before she acts.

M.O.B is consciousness, so there is no room for any confusion, because a confused mind is a blind mind, an ignorant mind. M.O.B is awareness. Awareness ties in with consciousness; it's the sense of knowing. You can't deceive a person about something they "know."

M.O.B is strength. Strength this power, and power is truth. It takes more than lies to break a woman whose strength is in the power of truth.

M.O.B is consciousness. M.O.B is awareness, M.O.B is strength, and M.O.B is mind over body.

Mind over body, or the abbreviation, M.O.B/
Is to have your thoughts above your troubles to feel at ease./
A state of peace that allows you to feel so free./
Problems could be in your face and you still won't see./
Queen of light, you'll shine even when the sun leaves./
When times get cold, you'll make it so none freeze./
When the air gets thick, you'll breathe when none breathe./
Knowing the most important things in life are physically unseen./
Like love and loyalty, to open your eyes so you can see./
Who you are, and maybe you'll believe you can be./
The woman with her M.O.B who only achieves./
Above obstacles that trap your soul and lead you asleep./
M.O.B - the spark that'll start every flame./
As it runs through your body and you feel it in every vein./
If you have your M.O.B, then you'll never be plain./
With the power to bring pleasure to every pain./
Putting angels at the door of your mind, you settle in./
Shutting out the chaos of life, not letting the devil in./
Even if he got through, there's no chance he'll ever win./
Because having your M.O.B will make you stronger than you've ever been./
M.O.B - the indication that you know something./

Searching For Souls

The inspiration that keeps your mind, body, and soul pumping./
To beat down negative thoughts like they stole something./
To chase after your dreams like they owe something./
Be serious and realize life's more than a hobby./
Sometimes you have to carry the load until your shoulders are popping./
Keep the thought in your mind, "No soldier can stop me."/
You're already somebody; just put your mind over body./

Mikal Bethea

Growing Pains

    Growing pains start out as irritations and grow into life changes. It's the small things you must deal with in the early stages, because when you ignore and overlook them, they act as diseases.
    Thus, they multiply, grow bigger and are no longer small things. And before you know it, you are surrounded by giants that grew from growing pains.

Emotional pains and physical pains are one in the same./
But, these pains can be misunderstood in the frame of the brain./
This brings frustration because pain can be hard to change./
But they won't change in a day because they didn't start in a day./
They are like seeds planted when you were bodily pure./
The small things you overlooked, thinking you got to be sure./
The same things causing confusion will probably lure./
You into a state of mind that's stopping the cure./
It's not good to let problems grow until they become extreme./
Because you must always fight with the best means./
But when small things can pierce your armor, what does a vest mean?/
Absolutely nothing and a brick wall will be what every guess seems./
You must be able to find comfort when family and the rest leave./
Because stress will make it hard to sleep when rest leaves./
Mind, body, and soul, you must continue to check these./
Because when times get cold, they'll be the best sleeves./
Pain can be unbearable, especially when sown in deceit./
Because they're lies to the soul that grow and repeat./
Can't win a war against pain when all you know is defeat./
But it brings joy to the heart when the soul is complete./
So cut off growing pains while they are all at your feet./
And cover up the holes in your life before they cause you to fall./
Everything standing in your way once had to crawl./
And every great fighter in history once had to brawl./
So put your hands up before you go insane./
Use your mind as an umbrella because you know it rains./
Be intelligent and remain strong until things slowly change./
To fight against being a victim of growing pains./

Life is What You Make it

The situation and circumstances your life is in didn't happen overnight. These things came into existence by a series of events. No one wakes up one morning to find his or her lives all of a sudden in shambles, no matter how much it may seem that way.

Your position in life "started" from somewhere, but it's up to you to decide the "stopping" point. You must kill all the things empowering your situation, and begin a new "starting" point for better living.

You have to begin a new lifestyle. That means a new way of thinking, a new way of speaking, and a new way of acting. For every action, there is a reaction. Meaning, what you put into something is what you get out, thus providing that life is what you make it.

Life is what you make it, but who can say it's perfectly./
With the trials and tribulations, we face in adversity./
On this path, a lot of women are not where they deserve to be./
And to be a witness watching this is constantly hurting me./
Life can be a doctor, to cut you away from your soul like surgery./
And it can certainly be a pool of doubt and uncertainty./
But if you believe you are queen, then life will worship thee./
To decree your every desire, like working bees./
It can be new air to your soul, like every time a person breathes./
Bring comfort when a person leaves or make every person dream./
To take away the panic in times of any emergency./
Or cause you to reach inside yourself to what searching brings./
But this all depends on how you allow life's problems to pressure you./
Because pressure busts pipes, and that's a force of life that measures you./
And some things that bring pain can bring pleasure too./
If you can learn how to face them to make a better you./
Don't take yourself for granted; you must be the one to treasure you./
Because if you don't, life will only dish out lesser dues./
Life can be your wings to help you fly like feathers do./

Mikal Bethea

Or bring comfort to your mind, body, and soul like leather shoes./
Sometimes life gets hard, but I'm bringing you better news./
Whatever you do, never quit, and you'll most likely never lose./
Life will be filled with rain if you let the weather choose./
So take control of your life like most people will do./
Because in life's equation, this can be a hard time or vacation./
But it's only hard for women who die trying to escape it./
If they would search their souls and strive to face it./
They'd come to the realization that life is what you make it./

Be Careful of What You Say

Many people, in general, don't believe their words have power, when in all actuality, your words can determine your failure or success.

For example, if you continually keep telling yourself, *"I am an overcomer!"* Eventually, you'll start believing it, or if you are like some insecure women who tell themselves, *"I'm not pretty,"* or, *"life's too hard,"* eventually, you'll start believing that too and start acting off it.

To find out what a person is thinking, just let them talk a lot. Because your words are a manifestation of your thoughts, or in other words, your words are formed in your mind, then spoken from your mouth.

Words are powerful. They start as thoughts and then change to words. Words are sounds, sounds are vibrations, and vibrations are a form of energy.

Energy surrounds us; it can be positive or negative. It's what a lot of people call a "vibe." The energy you send out is the same that will return. So be careful of what you say.

I've heard women speak negative things without any resistance./
Or any repentance and their words are really relentless./
Not realizing life won't change until the day that they get this./
That the most powerful women are those who speak things into existence./
Words can be used to help, or they "can" be to hurt./
So never say you can't make it because that "can" be a curse./
See, your words are like clothes, and they "can" be a shirt./
Or they can be your life jacket when your arms and hands can't work./
Most times it's no good to be talking too plain./
Don't always speak your two cents; sometimes you have to keep your loose change./
Words are sparks of energy, bringing forth new flames./
To burn down roads and the path of life has two lanes./
In one lane, you have success and the things that it brings./
Joy, happiness, and wealth to put in the face of a queen./

Mikal Bethea

But in the other lane is failure, and in any case, it will seem./
Like you're running in place instead of chasing your dreams./
I can search your soul, but you must seek for yourself./
I say good things in poems, much wisdom, but you must speak for yourself./
Bad words are like diseases that seek for your death./
To blow your lungs in front of your body and make you reach for your breath./
So let your words be positive, and they'll, therefore, be a place./
You can call your refuge to be there for you every day./
Like heaven on earth, so lovely for you to stay./
So be aware of what you think and always be careful of what you say./

You're Only a Woman

Women are the most precious things God put on this earth. There is absolutely nothing I can bring in comparison with them; gold and diamonds can't compare. Because gold only looks good and a diamond is only a pretty rock, literally!

But women don't only look good, they "are" good; good for living, good for commitment, and good for a man's soul. Women are more than just ornaments of gold and diamonds because you can put a price on those things, but women are priceless.

Priceless, without them there would be no "us." They're the ones who give birth to new life, and all human life, showing that even though most men are physically stronger than them, they possess a strength far greater in child labor.

So there you have it, just a small example of your beauty, your strength, and your importance. So, never let anyone tell you anything different unless it's another compliment.

So, when problems come your way, when life comes at you from all angles, don't sweat. Just remind yourself, you are only a woman.

In some situations, you may feel you're ducking at calls./
When life's screaming, throwing obstacles that have you ducking at balls./
Some women don't even duck, they take it with no fussing at all./
Not knowing what to do, they do nothing at all./
But you must open your eyes and see what's unmistakable./
Which is the fact that what you're going through its inescapable./
Because you have the power to succeed in any place you go./
And you're worth as a woman is irreplaceable./
To the point heads turn as you're leading the road./
Waiting for you to conquer over life and get your feet in control./
If life was a movie, I know you would be leading a role./
You are what you eat, so lady, what are you feeding your soul?/
See, you have to hold yourself better than you've been held./
If it was impossible, you would've been failed, tripped over life, and been fell./
Life's an ocean, so go get your boat together and then sail./

Mikal Bethea

Breathe and inhale, even when it seems like you're in hell./
Don't be afraid; force yourself to look through heights./
Stay on the straight path, even when left looks too right./
Let confidence envelope you like theft crooks do night./
And don't panic when what you've felt hooks too tight./
Your future will be better than your past if you're present is part of it./
Life's a puzzle; can you say your pieces are a part of it?/
Break every problem down until you reach the heart of it./
And destroy what's in front of you without the speech of an argument./

Push It to the Limit

My grandmother once told me, "If you're going to do something, don't play around with it; do it!" Now I'm passing that along to you. If you're setting out goals in life, don't half step; give it your all.

When you half step, you get half results. Never focus on how hard it is. There's nothing in life that is worth having that's easy to get. Stay motivated, stay on the move, show and prove, and be sure to push it to the limit.

To fail or to succeed, some women don't or might care./
And stop when their prize results are right there./
But you must breathe, and make sure it's the right air./
And chase your dreams before you wake up standing in a nightmare./
From the day your mother bore you, the doctor said, "Keep pushing!"/
You took your first breath and your mind told your heart, *"Keep pumping!"*/
It was a struggle, and in every struggle, you seek something./
Got to beat something, so when you feel like you can't go any further, keep pushing./
Don't go through all that pain just to give up in the end./
When storms come, let your confidence build up with the wind./
Not everything that's born will live much in the end./
Because some people achieve desires while others pretend./
And that's tragic, but to some women, that life's just average./
To see a hole in their lives and be too lazy to patch it./
So gain passion, because anything you want in life, you can have it./
Just have the motivation it takes with the mind state to match it./
So when the heat comes you don't have to melt like plastic./
When life comes enchanted you'll just step like magic./
Push it to the limit, and fight like a savage./
Be charismatic, enthusiastic, and know you are the baddest./
Because the only thing you'll get out of life is what you give it./
And you'll only get the "whole" package if you finish./

Mikal Bethea

Life's different for different women, so how will you spend it?/
No matter how it looks in the beginning, just push it to the limit./

There's a Season for Everything

There's a season for everything in life. From the beginning, there is a season for birth, then the season for growth, and the season for death. Nothing lives forever on earth.

But in between those seasons are a lot more. For example, there's a season for storms, when the reality of life kicks in and you realize you won't always live as a child but will grow and have the many responsibilities of an adult.

You go through those storms. Then a season of experience comes. Inside the season of experience, you have a season of falls, a season of gaining knowledge, and a season of gaining strength. Even after these, it is the season of becoming a woman. It is up to you to decide "what kind" of woman you will be.

You see, there is a season for everything. You even have seasons for certain seasons. These will be with you until the day you pass away. They are just like the seasons of the earth; they come and go but always return. Some are worse than others are; some do not last as long as others do. Overall, you can believe there is a season for everything.

Everything in life will eventually have its season./
And time to express itself and expand its region./
The effects of each season may come as a legion./
But it's up to you to find out what is its reason./
Some women can't stand stormy seasons coming from the skies./
Living in lies like life is something to disguise./
My message to them all is, stop running from your life./
With thoughts running through your mind and tears running from your eyes./
Because this is only a season, a light reminder./
Something that will hopefully make your life finer./
If you're looking for the woman in you, search your soul; you might find her./
Then let it adorn you like lipstick and eyeliner./
When it's finalized, look yourself in the mirror and apologize./
For all the contributions you made to emotional homicide./
Those things can dramatize and bring stress to a lot of eyes./

Mikal Bethea

So stand up and provide, because you've got to provide./
Seasons can be wake up calls of truth to kill the best of lies./
And bring a sense of purpose to the rest of lives./
Go so hard that you leave other people mesmerized./
So they'll know beauty and strength can stand the test of time./
There's an umbrella that can protect you from every rain./
And help ease the hurt you feel from every pain./
They say some people will try to make reasons for everything./
I guess "some people" know there is a season for everything./

Appreciation of Rain

Most times when we as people go through things, we focus more on the situation than on what we can gain from it, and thus, we lose that which we could've gained. We become so focused on how bad the pain is that we divert our attention from gaining more strength.

We also complain more about situations than we tried to do something about them. We complain about everything going wrong, not acknowledging what's right, and not realizing that what's wrong can be made to help better us.

When you catch a cold, your throat gets scratchy, your nose runs, you catch a bad cough, etc. These symptoms will turn most people against them, but there actually on your side.

There letting you know "something" is wrong with your body. These symptoms aren't what's "really" wrong. They are the only "effects" of the real problem.

In addition, most people do not realize the medicine they are taking is only killing the symptoms, not the cold. These symptoms are only letting you know, and you are killing the messenger, not the enemy. So appreciate the symptoms, because, without them, you would not know.

It's the same with the storms in your life. You must learn to embrace the rain. It's the rain that shows you how much you can take, showing you your strength. The rain gave you the understanding that life is not always easy. So it gave you a reality check, shaking you out your dream state.

The rain made you appreciate the sunshine when it came back around. So, not everything bad has intentions. Call it tough love if you will. But, learn to have an appreciation of rain.

Dark clouds always come at the wrong time when they start down./
It's quiet before the storm comes, and you can't hear far sounds./
The only sound you'll hear in your ear is that beat every time your heart pounds./
Then the clouds so high in the sky start to cry in the rain falls down./
It might drizzle then stop, then rain some more./

Mikal Bethea

Then it comes down harder, faster, and when it rains, it pours./
And the place that you thought was a house, is the place that changed its doors./
Not letting you in, afraid that the rain might stain the floor./
So the rain falls for five hours, six hours, then seven./
But is it bad rain, or God opening the floodgates of the heavens?/
To help you, raise you, show you, and teach you a lesson./
And in the end, what you went through is the same thing that blesses./
I have respect for you, and all these storms are only testing you./
Like lessons do, so never let them get the best of you./
Seek the answer to everything you have a question to./
You know your physical, but what about the importance of the rest of you?/
Rain will soak even the high places when it comes there./
So you have to make your soul a shelter and run there./
It won't rain forever, but it thunders long before it's done there./
But always remember, when it's raining, the sun is still shining somewhere./
Sometimes it takes water to see the places of pain./
To heal the bruises, and turn them into pieces praying for gain./
Prayers are answered, and they'll never leave places the same./
To the point you'll show appreciation of rain./

New Life Through Death

In Egyptian mythology, there is the story of the phoenix, a red-feathered beautiful bird. The story of the phoenix tells how the bird lived for five hundred years then burned itself out. Literally, set himself on fire with flames from within its own body. And when it burned itself to nothing more than ashes, it arose from those ashes as a baby bird. Rebirth, a new phoenix, renewed from the ashes of its old self, to live another five hundred years.

That's how you must do yourself. Your old self must die off in order for your new life to begin. You can't say you want your life to change, and still cling on to your old ways. It won't work. How can you want to live a happy life, but you're always depressed? How can you want to be wealthy, but you're never trying to take steps in getting money?

When gold is refined, it is put in a pot, which is then heated by the fire until it melts to liquid form. In its liquid form, it separates from any other minerals in it. So, engulf yourself in flames, and separate yourself from anything holding you back. Shed off all the negativity and let it burn to ashes, and then rebirth yourself like the phoenix, to bring forth new life through death.

Life is a book, but you have to read for self./
If you can't, then it's best to go seek help./
Success is a promise to all who sow their seeds of wealth./
Because in life, the only thing guaranteed is death./
So you must die many times and resurrect in the course of a savior./
To save your soul in belief and speech in the voice of creators./
To create a new you and rejoice in the favor./
Life is like a box of chocolates, but most don't enjoy the flavors./
If you want your life to change, it's a must that you change you./
Don't hold on to the rope of your past, it will eventually hang you./
With the same view, unable to see and seek things through./
So in a sense, your hands have become false makers./
When your old self should've died off, and let death be a fault taker./
To take away flaws, because this life can be a heartbreaker./

Mikal Bethea

To talk later, and spill you over like salt shakers./
In order to change, you have to learn to fight./
Because what feels good today, might burn tonight./
So pick your head up and turn your sight, though the sun is bright./
It takes away darkness to return the light./
And that light is life, a brand new life you've felt./
A new hand from a deck of cards two lives have dealt./
Always be the type to do right to self./
Then perform the miracle of bringing new life through death./

Traditional Thinking

There was once a family named the McCoy's, a middle-class people who liked simple living.

One Thanksgiving, five-year-old Jamesha McCoy was watching her mother prepare the turkey. When her mother put the turkey in the pan, she tied its wings and legs together.

Upon seeing this, Jamesha asked, "Mom, why do you tie the turkey's wings and legs together?"

Her mother replied, "This is the way my momma did it, so this is how I do it."

So, Jamesha ran from the kitchen to her grandmother's room. Approaching her grandmother, Jamesha asked her the same question she asked her mother.

Her grandmother replied, "Because, that's the way my mama did it so that's the way I do it. You can call it tradition."

Then, Jamesha ran to the living room where her great grandmother was sitting in a rocking chair. She asked the same question she asked her mother and grandmother.

Her grandmother chuckled and said, "Child, that ain't no tradition. When your grandma was a child, we were so poor; we tied the turkey because our pan was too small for it to fit in!"

This is an example of traditional thinking. Jamesha's mother and grandmother were clinging on to something they "thought" had a meaning to it when it meant nothing. However, they had seen it done so many times, that it became a custom to them. They didn't want to tear away from it; they were programmed.

It's the same way with poverty and a lot of other struggles in life. You see it done so much until it becomes normal. It's all you know. Your mother barely makes ends meet and struggle to survive. So you feel it's normal for your life to be so.

Your mother was beat on by her husband, and so was her mother. So you both see it as your fault when your husbands beat on you. You must break the cycle and therefore, end that traditional thinking.

In many cases, women are living without a dream in sight./

Mikal Bethea

Stuck in the same box as those before them, and can't leave the site./
Momma didn't make it out of grandma's shadow, so they believe alike./
But, just because mama did it doesn't mean it's right./
Traditional thinking can be a cage or a fortress./
Knights and horses, but for most, it becomes a forest./
Running in the ways of those before you will leave you seeking for rest./
Confused and gasping for air as you reach for your chest./
So you must make your own steps in life like plenty do./
Because it's bad to accept things from any view./
Set out a course to a destination that's fitting "you."/
Then make sure where you're going in life is worth getting to./
Use observation; think before you act through contemplation./
Think outside of the box, and the move beyond the basics./
A lot of patience; speak things into your life like conversation./
Ambition is the fire that constantly burns the soul./
To the degree that everything you touch turns to gold./
There is no refund to return what's sold./
So you can never lose anything that concerns the soul./
So get it and sound off like a whistle is ringing./
And bring peace of mind, no matter how the system is seeming./
Don't base your life off the wrong individual's thinking./
Because then you're repeating their mistakes through traditional thinking./

Stand Right There

Struggles in life can be counted as strong winds. These strong winds aren't necessarily bad things. They can be made into stepping-stones. You can use these things to make you better.

But, these winds can also break you if you let them. The key word is "if." Because, just like growing pains, these winds grow too. And if you ignore them for too long, they'll grow into tornadoes and hurricanes.

If you get caught in one of these, it is extremely difficult to escape, because they twist you up, spin your thoughts, and throw you around until you lose almost complete control over your life. But, not all hope is lost.

You can use your mental strength to push against the momentum of these winds. But why let it get that far? Why not stop them in their early stages of small winds? Don't let them grow.

Think of this: in order for a tornado to grow, it must be isolated. They need the room. So, compare this room to space in your mind. Most tornadoes and hurricanes start in the ocean, where they are not disturbed and have good room and time to build up. Now compare the ocean to your thoughts.

Don't give these struggles or winds enough room inside your mind. Don't allow them to grow stronger in your thoughts, or ocean, because they'll spin your thoughts to the point you can't think when faced with adversity.

Remain strong physically, mentally, and spiritually, and don't crumble. Let the winds pass and break apart when they reach you, and stand right there.

What do you do when the winds blow and blocking air?/
When you can't breathe, grab your chest and feel a knocking there./
And it's not stopping there. Would you do nothing but stop and stare?/
As winds knock your life back and forth like rocking chairs./
Bells stop ringing, but you still know the song./
Won't acknowledge the problems, but you still know the wrong./

Mikal Bethea

Winds that carry rocks will eventually throw a stone./
Have you around a crowd of people, but still feel so alone./
These winds will grow, and maybe, in the end, you'll know./
Your relationship with obstacles are they a friend or foe?/
If they are friends, they'll help you, and in the end, you'll grow./
If they are foes, it'll be seeds of defeat the winds will sow./
But it's up to you to decide, so which way will you lie?/
To help you again, or help you fail, while waving you bye./
Manage your life from pain that's making you cry./
Because the way that you live will be the way that you die./
Think positive and keep your mind straight even through confusion./
Because winds can make your eyes blurry and have you seeing illusions./
Peace and happiness, you must keep thinking of such conclusions./
And you'll make it through the storm with minor cuts and bruises./
Reach for the stars, and keep your hands right there./
In the midst of winds, reach for control, and keep your hands right there./
To the point time stops, and every man might stare./
When winds blow, stay founded on faith, and stand right there./

The Caged Birds

From being in prison, I experienced many things. However, one thing I can comprehend most is being caged. I know what it feels like to be locked in a room for 24 hours a day. I know the feeling of being abandoned when everyone leaves you on your own when you've cried so much you can't cry anymore. When it feels like the walls are closing in on you. I know the feeling of depression, sadness, and stress. I know.

So I understand the pain your soul feels when it's caged, locked away in a prison of oppression, waiting to break free and spread its wings to express itself to the world.

The worst part about all things said, is the person keeping it bound is the one closest to it, and that's you. If you are boxing your soul, you are your worst enemy.

So, you have to think outside the box to free what's inside the box. Drop and destroy the walls surrounding your soul. Hack into whom you are to find out what you can do in life. After that, decide what you want and how to get it. Then, go get it! First, release the caged bird.

I never understood why a person would put a bird in a cage./
The representation of freedom, that deserves to be staged./
And placed high to sing what we've heard in this age./
But instead, it's hurting in shame./
It's a shame when the bird is your soul, hoping the deeds come./
To bring peace and space, because it really needs some./
To be free to go, free to come, whenever the need comes./
It's sad when you can pay your way out of jail, but you can't buy freedom./
Your life's surrounded by fire, and you hurry the flames./
But there is no grave deep enough to bury the pain./
No part of this earth will allow you to bury the shame./
You've felt oppression, but release is also worthy to gain./
You give to others, but to yourself do you give enough?/
Life has a price, but you can't afford not to live it up./
Freedom is priceless; you should never want to give it up./
Even if it costs the world, your soul is still enough./

Mikal Bethea

You want to succeed, but you are so close to fail./
Your souls in jail, and it seems like you are so close to hell./
The pressures of life will break you if your bones are frail./
Time is true because time is known to tell./
So break free, and let freedom be every day's word./
Express your soul like a book and make every page heard./
Acts of faith, and bring life to everything you gave words./
Then use life as the key to release the caged bird./

One Step at a Time

    Sometimes it seems like the troubles in life always come in pairs, like, maybe you are blessed with a beautiful baby. But, you have to feed and clothe babies. Then, you have to put and keep a roof over their heads.
    So now, you'll need a job. And if you don't live in a big city to ride a train or bus, you will need a car.
    This is just an example of how one thing can lead to another until after a while you'll have multiple things on your plate.
    Most people struggling in these positions try to carry them all at one time. The result is they becoming overwhelmed with burdens and falling.
    As things fall and crash around them, they become desperate for solutions. They become miserable, stressed out, or worse, suicidal.
    So, do not panic, take it one day at a time. Solving problems one by one, eventually, they will go down in number. Become experienced, and learn how to juggle two or three at a time. But, until you become that skilled, just take it one step at a time.

Life hits hard and unexpected from all kinds of angles./
To mix you up and have your thoughts in all kinds of tangles./
Worrying about too many things will leave your mind unstable./
And drop you to your knees, praying for all kinds of angels./
Pure pressure in a war you are having a fight./
Blinded by clouds of doubt that are passing your sight./
But, hope is out there, flickering like a flash of light./
To help you shine, when your dark moods are matching the night./
Crawl before you walk, and provide help to your plan./
Like someone holding out their arms to help you stand./
Problems come, but you can solve them, so step if you can./
Until they fade away like footprints left in the sand./
Take them one at a time don't let them gang up./
That's dangerous. They'll beat your life and leave it banged up./
To make you change up and do nothing but hang up./
When you should've locked hands with your soul and trust./
You can make it; I wrote this book to show you how./

Mikal Bethea

To add my pearls of wisdom with those you've found./
Keep your mind straight don't let burdens fold you down./
Or slow you down, you've come too far to let them hold you now./
Keep pushing; don't let your eyes melt from the prize./
That's when you're losing focus, don't step to the side./
Your race won't begin or end until you step to the line./
But don't rush it. Just take it one step at a time./

When It All Falls Down

I don't want to mislead you in this book. I don't want you to be thinking that life is all sunny days because that's not the case. Life gets hard, sometimes very hard, but not impossible.

Therefore, with this in mind, you must be prepared. There is nothing wrong with having a Plan B, or even a Plan C. That's called, preparing for the worst, and hoping for the best. Better yet, prepare for the worst and "work" for the best.

Because there is always the possibility of something going wrong, whether that possibility is big or small, it's still there, and just like a game of chess, one wrong move can lead to two wrong moves, then ultimately, disaster.

So, all I'm saying is, don't plan to fall but prepare to fall. That way, it won't affect you as much. Think about it, what would hurt the worse? Something you can see and prepare for or something that's unexpected?

It's just like putting a helmet, knee pads, elbow pads, etc. on your child before riding a bike. You don't "want" them to fall, but you want them to be "prepared" to fall to limit the harm done when it all falls down.

Sometimes you can get caught in illusions as your brain is soaring./
When it seems nothing can go wrong to change the morning./
So you're left vulnerable as clouds in range are forming./
And you're unexpectedly soaked as the rain is pouring./
Do you see how things can suddenly change in your territory?/
When you're caught off guard, thinking life will be forever glory./
But when it all falls down, you can make it a better story?/
Not every movie made is promised a sequel./
Hurricanes have hit cities to demolish the people./
So be prepared as the clock ticks to astonish the peaceful./
Because time will make liars out of some of the most honest people./
When those people make claims with no expression of proof./
Trying to change reality by stretching the truth./
But power will only be gained through access to the truth./

Mikal Bethea

Because truth will set you free at the best of its use./
What will you do when your hearts gripped by the hands of stress?/
When things get out of line, will you demand respect?/
Because you can't rewind time once the hands are set./
So take hold of your life, and make sure your hands are set./
Because you'll need strong hands when the ball falls down./
And you need to hold yourself up when the walls fall down./
Be prepared in the dark when you're hearing small sounds./
That way it won't hurt as much when it all falls down./

Exaggeration

The word exaggeration means, to make greater than is actually the case, to overstate. That is exactly what is done in many situations.

When going through challenging circumstances, some women tend to make matters worse by stressing, and the problem becomes an illusion of something it isn't.

It's the same with small things as well. The problem can be so easy to solve, but due to all else that's going on, it becomes big.

When your mind can't come up with an immediate answer, you get frustrated. Frustration leads to aggravation, and then aggravation leads to anger, and no one can think straight when they are angry.

All this started from stress, which feeds off exaggeration. So to avoid this, what you have to do is stay in tune with reality, because when you exaggerate, you're actually deceiving yourself, painting a false picture.

Don't let the problem grow bigger than it already is in your mind. If it's small, let it remain small. If it's big, don't lose sense of reality, remain calm and focused, and take your time. Don't be led away by exaggeration.

Situations flip in life at the toss of a dime./
Flipping you mentally every time they cross with the mind./
Because That's where they're able to grow through loss of the time./
The same time you spent exaggerating to exhaust the mind./
There's only so much dirt 24 hours a day brings./
But that doesn't mean you have to solve it all at once to stay clean./
Because that's when exaggeration comes into play to make things./
Impossible, when they're not as big as they may seem./
Open your eyes and realize, life will only be life if you live it./
Struggles come with time, but don't get stuck for hourless minutes./
Time is sweet, so don't let exaggeration sour the minutes./

Mikal Bethea

Because the problem you have will only have the power you give it./
So don't exaggerate, allow your thoughts to navigate./
Don't focus on what you can't change, and fight what you have to face./
Sometimes you have to pray in order to make matters safe./
When things get bittersweet, leaving a bad aftertaste./
Most of all, be prepared; never be scared./
Every cause has its effects, and they'll forever be pairs./
Exaggeration brings stress, and peace will never be there./
So when you feel yourself slipping, you better beware./
Being to fire is what will connect you to your aspirations./
Which are the things that inspire you to make it./
But in order to make it, you must have patience./
And a foundation that won't allow you to be led by exaggeration./

Torn Between the Two

When you're faced with adversity, there's always two roads. You can go backward or forward, fight or surrender, fail or succeed. It's a double-edged sword, and these two are always in the back of your mind.

It's so easy to give up and give in, because when you're climbing a hill, it takes no effort to roll backward. When you're swimming, it takes more to stay afloat than to let yourself sink to the bottom. So, it doesn't take much to take the easy way out, the coward's way out.

But, to win, it takes courage, which is to master your fear. Fear of failure, fear of loss, fear of hurt, or any other type of fear. In order to overcome, it takes strength to overpower your faults. It takes confidence in self not to "think" you can do it, but to "know."

So, your mind is constantly stuck between these two the whole time you're going through, asking questions like, "Is it worth it? Should I stop now? Can I really make it?"

Well, I say, if you truly want something, then yes, it is worth it. Yes, you can make it. But, sometimes, until you get it, your mind will stay torn between the two.

Every destination has two ways onto the road./
Success that shines bright, and failure that lays into a hole./
Hoping to make you slip as doubt fades into your soul./
So, you don't know if you should stay, or if you should go./
It's real to say, even though obstacles are still in the way./
You must keep going because even Rome wasn't built in a day./
Ignore all you want, but the thoughts are still in your face./
Asking which side of this hill will you take?/
The easy way that goes down descending onto?/
The place you started in the beginning confused./
Which way will you take? There's nothing standing defending the two./
But, keep in mind everything and everyone depending on you./
Maybe it's your kids, and you know you must survive for them./
Because, if you're not there, then who'll provide for them?/

Mikal Bethea

Choose wisely, an outcome will be born between the two./
Lean towards success, and never be torn between the two./

Choices and Consequences

I once asked an elder I was incarcerated with this question, "What is life about?"

He looked me in the eye and replied, "Choices and consequences."

I agree those are absolutely two important concepts.

Decisions, decisions, decisions, the decisions you make will determine your tomorrow.

If you are stuck in a tight position, and you decide to do something illegal and get caught, you have to live with those consequences. If you choose to spend your money on materialistic things, not taking care of your needs, you have to live with those consequences.

If you choose to put trust in someone deceitful and they stab you in the back, you have to live with those consequences. If you choose to have unprotected sex with someone you barely know, and you are left with a disease, you have to live with those consequences.

This is your life, so choose wisely, and always remember life is all about choices and consequences.

The choices you made in the past determine where you are today./
But for some to admit it's their fault is hard to say./
You'll forget about small things that seem so far away./
But those same small things contributed to who you are today./
Everyone makes mistakes, but you only get one pass percentage./
Because the first time it's a mistake, after that, it's a bad decision./
The choices you make will either lead you to rags or riches./
Or a sad position if you choose with bad intentions./
Maybe you had the vision, but it wasn't strapped like a leather vest./
Or you choose wisely in one area, but never the rest./
The best thing about choices is you can turn them all together for the best./
And choose to make every choice better than the next./
You can change your life from chaos to an orderly place./
But first, you must make the choice to get your priorities straight./

Mikal Bethea

Bad decisions will cost you, but it will take more to replace./
The strength of your foundation in order for your floor to be safe./
The floor of your home, your home is the core of your soul./
So realize you need your soul more than you know./
Because that's where you'll find peace the more you grow./
In this river of dreams we call life it's the core of your hope./
As you row upstream against all odds, you must listen./
To sounds that warn you of voices of opposition./
You can choose to make them nothing but voices without a vision./
As you live life, which is all about choices and consequences./

What's Best for You

You have women who go all their lives giving to others. Some do this in order to hope they will please others like they are inferior or lower than others and like the happiness of their lives comes from the acceptance of another person's words.

If you are this type of woman, I want you to know that you should live your life for you. It's okay to look out for other people's interests, but "you" must be a top priority.

Sometimes you can do things for people, and in the end, you're the one taking a big loss. It's one thing to help people, but it's another when you allow yourself to be used.

I know these types are out there because I've seen it too many times. The big question is, "Why, why would you allow yourself to be used? Would that person do the same for you?"

Plus, if you do it once, they'll look for you to do it over and over again. So you have to learn to say "no" sometimes. It's not about being cold hearted or anything. But you must look out for your best interest, and do what's best for you.

I've seen women mistreat themselves in a number of ways./
Their bodies awake, but the soul's been in a slumber for days./
Wanting to shine, but the mind is standing under the rays./
In a storm controlled by others, who thunder the rain./
People will use you, and fool you into thinking you must have believed./
That you are only a servant, and life is nothing it seems./
Until you give into their words and what they esteem./
It's sad when the most beautiful women do the ugliest things./
Some people speak of their problems because they know you'll listen./
And go out of your way to give away when you know you'll miss it./
It pains my heart to see you with a hole in your vision./
It's true that some women will even sell their soul for attention./
But, don't let that be you; if it is, make it end this moment./
God gave you life as a gift, so, in the end, you own it./
People will place their mark like paper when a pen is on it./

Mikal Bethea

But let them know it's yours; don't pretend you want it./
Because if you do, you're fooling yourself on many things./
If you're not living for self, you're being withheld from many dreams./
You must have a foundation with a head of plenty steam./
Because if you stand for nothing, you'll fall for anything./
So guard your heart and soul, even if it takes a vest or two./
Set a good example to show how the rest should do./
Make it so you never have to guess or choose./
When it comes down to doing what's best for you./

Let It Go

You cannot expect to move forward in life when you're always focused on things that have happened in the past. Why? Because you can't give enough attention to what's in your face when you're stuck on what's behind you.

Bad things happen to many women; bad things have happened to you. But, the question is, "Can you move past it?" Can you tell yourself, "Okay, that happened in the past; that's where I'll leave it. It's over, and I'm done with it!"

So, someone says something negative to you that really affected you. Does that determine the outcome of your life? Someone you love passed away. Don't forget about them, but when will you stop mourning? When will you move on with your life?

These things are like ropes you are holding onto, and not matter what kind, every rope has its stopping point. If you're still holding onto it, that'll be your stopping point in life as well, so, let it go!

Life's a struggle, unpredictable in what it has present./
So powerful it has some women stuck in past events./
But you must learn to move past events./
Go on with your life. Don't let the past prevent./
Because if you do, you'll be headed for a fast descent./
Still questioning God about the task he sent./
In the future, you'll see it was the last he sent./
But will you be the first to fall, or the last to quit?/
Some women bottle up and put it under a lid./
But when that bottle bust, it exposes every summer you hid./
Every winter of sorrow, and what the thunder had did./
You held onto it, not letting it flow like water under a bridge./
Can't get over it, it's probably running through your mind right now./
Causing stress to envelope your whole body like a nightgown./
Closing your ears to how sweet melodies of life might sound./
Can't step forward, because what's behind wasn't the right ground./

Mikal Bethea

You have to be the woman who allowed her soul to search her./
Found herself with the power to hold and nurture./
Everything the future holds and makes life serve her./
And never allowing her past mistakes to hurt her./
I know you're reading, but are you getting the message, though?/
I just want you to find your light and let it show./
But you won't find that light if you never met the soul./
You can't change what's done in the past, so let it go!/

The Butterfly Effect

When caterpillars are born, they are referred to as larva, which is their description in wingless form. But, one day, they will come to the realization that they are more than "just" caterpillars.

That's when they go through their metamorphosis stages and envelope themselves into what is called a pupa or cocoon, which is basically a shell, and from within that shell, they emerge as beautiful butterflies.

You must go through in life this same metamorphosis. The caterpillar is a representation of a lost woman, one who is only "surviving" life and not living it. The caterpillar is like a zombie walking around aimlessly. And that's another representation of a woman who's asleep, one whose unconscious of who and what she really is.

But when the caterpillar becomes aware and awake, it stops. Then it tells itself, *"Hold up. I'm a butterfly!"* Then it goes through the necessary process of becoming a butterfly.

So must you. You must come to terms with the power of knowing who you are and what you can do. Go inside yourself like the caterpillar inside the pupa, and search your soul, then emerge that beautiful conscious woman you are. And manifest the butterfly effect.

You can be so consumed with problems that you can't focus on self./
Like a person who's sleepwalking and only knows to go left./
Instead of right, doing right when life has a rope on the step./
That wraps around your lungs to make you choke on your breath./
Trying to gain purpose when you don't know who you are./
But consciousness will grow more and more the stronger you are./
Until you shine so bright that everyone knows you're a star./
Making their vision clearer and clearer the closer you are./
But you won't accomplish this when "you're" the one in the dark./
Not ready to change errors that were done from the start./
Blind people don't know where to step when life's coming apart./
So you have to bring light to everything done in the dark./
By searching your soul and transforming yourself further ahead./

Mikal Bethea

Into the mind of a queen, and men will start to worship your head./
No words can describe the woman who bears what she said./
And realizes that she's more than what her worth is said./
But you'll only become this woman if you choose to./
Change from the ways and everything that you're used to./
And never go back to living life the way you used to./
Because that is one thing that will confuse you./
So, free what you hold and cover by the rest./
Then become that which none other can reflect./
Unless they go through the same process, then another might detect./
The attributes of the woman born from the butterfly effect./

Tears of Life

There are many different types of tears. Some people shed tears when they become overjoyed and happy; they become overwhelmed by emotions. Some people shed tears over the simplest matters. But, inside their minds, the situation is great. Then you have tears of sorrow, and I believe we all have experienced these.

You also have tears of stress when times seem so hard, and you don't know what to do when you can't find an answer. Then when it feels like nothing else can go wrong, something goes wrong. When frustration sets in and you feel like pulling your hair out and all you can do is cry.

Well cry, let it all out. Don't hold it in. That will only contribute to you having a nervous breakdown. Holding those emotions in will require pressure and pressure burst pipes. And when those pipes burst, they're hard to repair.

But don't only cry, you do that to relieve stress. After you've calmed down, break your situation down piece by piece. Do something to better your circumstances. Because "just" crying isn't going to solve the problem. So don't get stuck in depression. Learn how to use and grow from the tears of life.

The impact of life feels like a slap when the truth hits./
When the problems you face seem like traps that are too thick./
Like hands that grip tight and squeeze like two fist./
Then pull and twist until your mind snaps like toothpicks./
Now the life that was so sweet has taken a strange taste./
As the pressure builds, you wonder how much can the brain take./
Before the picture of life loses color and the frame breaks./
Making you want to give up, lose hope, and change faith./
So you cry tears that will cover and stain space./
Being locked down in your position, just hoping the chain breaks./
It's a plain day when pain plays in vain for name's sake./
As tears map your face like roads that always lead to the same place./
Everyone has a breaking point in the tails of their lives./
A hard place to land as they fell from their pride./

Mikal Bethea

As their vision went blurry, and eyes fell from the prize./
And the tears of life filled up the wells of their eyes./
And they cried, so this is when you let it out the most./
Empty yourself of pressure, and try not to choke./
As tears march down your face as silent as smoke./
In the belly of the beast, fight, and come out the throat./
So don't just cry, you have to face your fears of life./
Come up with a plan for victory, and cheers tonight./
Don't stress yourself out, use your ears for sight./
Whenever your eyes get cloudy from crying the many tears of life./

Alone but not Lonely

Many women are unable to stand alone, depending on others to survive or stay happy. As crazy as this statement may seem, it's true: "the average person can't stand to be around themselves for too long."

Sometimes that's what you need, to be alone by yourself in solitude, to be able to learn more about you to gain an understanding of yourself and why you do the things you do.

We can sit down, observe, and analyze others all day, but can you break down your own mental behavior? It's sad how a person can know so much about others but know nothing about themselves.

It's easy to gossip and give an opinion about someone's else's life but depressing to face the cold hard facts of your own. It's called being a coward.

When you are afraid to deal with yourself and your weaknesses, you're being a coward, not realizing, that by facing yourself and identifying weaknesses, you can turn them into strong points.

Solitude contributes to this because you're forced to confront yourself. So, don't "have" to depend on others, because what will you do when there is no one but you?

Learn to be comfortable with yourself. Take out time to be to yourself, even if it's only two hours a day because it's possible to be alone but not lonely.

Not too many women can stand in the dark and be still./
By themselves, not knowing that's the place where peace lives./
Life starts as a blank wall, but will yours ever be filled?/
With pictures of happiness, completion, and deep thrills?/
Some women look to others for answers to the right and the wrong./
But when told, they say, "I already knew that." Then excitement is gone./
My question is, "Why couldn't you come up with that advice on your own?"/
Then make it permanent in your life like writing in stone./

Mikal Bethea

Most people can't deal with living in solitude./
Can't stand to be around themselves, their faults, and problems too./
But, this is what it takes to fix what's wrong inside of you./
Even babies feel at home in the dark inside the womb./
You must be able to carry your burdens and never fumble./
When you're alone, speak with authority and never mumble./
Be able to pick "yourself" up whenever you stumble./
And strong enough to stand by yourself in the jungle./
Because you won't always have a shoulder to lean on when people choose to leave./
And you're forced to deal with the things you refuse to see./
You gain strength from the place you refuse to be./
But it's up to you to believe what you can truly achieve./
Sometimes you need to get away when home isn't homey./
To be able to sing and know that your song isn't phony./
At times, it can seem your soul is not flowing./
But, it's also possible for you to be alone but not lonely./

Waste No Time

If you took heed to these poems, that's a good thing, but these poems are only considered knowledgeable. Knowledge is the know-how, to know how to do something, or in other words, information.

But, now I need you to apply wisdom to all this. Because wisdom is the expression of knowledge, it is the activation of knowledge. It is to be able to apply what you know to how you live, which will make you a wise woman.

A wise woman isn't one who only "knows" things. She's a woman who exercises what she knows. And when wisdom is combined with knowledge, they bring forth understanding, which is to see things clearly for what they are, not what they appear to be, to search your soul and see who you are and not what you appear to be.

But do this today. Don't wait until tomorrow. Take a step to better your life and change it right now, because tomorrow isn't promised to anyone, So waste no time.

Only women of action will be able to change their situations./
In many cases, it takes more than just making statements./
If you talk the talk, walk the walk, no matter your placement./
Because this road you walk on will shape to the way that you pave it./
It's really basic, for some, that's hard to see./
Don't put walls around your soul, because they're hard to beat./
If you don't make the effort to swim when the waters are deep./
Eventually, you'll sink, making it hard to breathe./
To see your problems and do nothing, just seems too crazy./
And to tell the truth, some women are just too lazy./
Or they are too content with suffering maybe./
And I've witnessed too many women who've been suffering lately./
Time never sits still, it always continues to pace./
And times change like seasons as you continue to wait./
So how long will you continue to wait?/
The time for change is today, tomorrow isn't promised anyway./

Mikal Bethea

But life will only change when you change your frame of mind./
If you want better, then do better and break the binds./
That hold some women back in the chase of lives./
But if you really want to live, search your soul, and waste no time!/

Jerz-Queen

My Kings, peace be unto you. Surely, the queen didn't forget to pay homage to you; Robust champion, noble, proud, and fearless; Chieftains of our households and villages… Progenitors of our off springs, us black queen's love, support, and honor you. We witness your trials and tribulations. We identify with your pain; we acknowledge that no queen should ever attempt to emasculate our kings. We understand the frustration / anger and just want to reinforce just how proud we are of our kings. Keep pursuing your dreams, heads held high. Unification is our only salvation. Salute Black man, you are king.

Queens of mothers of civilization, it's our responsibility to encourage, support, and educate our young kings and queens. If they fail, we fail. Know / live your role. We have to be the backbones to our kings. If we don't protect them, who will, if we don't love them who will? If the foundation is weak, your house will crumble… Unite and build. Black man, you are a gift to the black woman, your strength is acknowledged, you are kings, warriors, intellectual beings, who deserve so much more than you've been given. Don't give up on us, we will never give up on you. United we stand, divided we fall. Queens I've seen the challenges we've all participated in. Now my challenge to you is, forever uphold our kings… Blessings.

Don't let your loyalty become slavery. Know when to let go and never compromise your self-respect.!

Tonya Thetakeover Cherry

Mikal Bethea

Daddy's Girl – Black Goddess

Listen, my daughter, too many young black girls are lost. Do not whiten your face.

Do not go outside your race.

You are my way back when I die. I want to come back black.

Listen, my daughter, I really miss that kinky African hair. Wear it proudly and be comfortable in your skin.

Only give man attention when he measures up to your father. Or else, this will be the both of our sins if you let a coward in!

Listen, my daughter, your body is made just like the mighty "Goddess ISIS," You may wanna show it off.

It is priceless!

No item or any amount of money can buy it.

No situation of life should you choose to go in body first.

Listen, my daughter to your father, mother of the universe, life will be the way you direct it, you were born to be a queen with beauty, substance, pride, integrity, a treasure. This is you Aiyana Phyllis Smith.

Written by BoBo
NWK, NJ. M.M.C Bricks

The Mirror

You look and say, "Why me?" You beat yourself down day after day. You play the blame game but never win. You don't like the pain. But, what will you do? People say this and that, but they are only speaking fact. Is this really love? No not doing stuff like that.

The New You

I was once out of control, could not see,
Did not know how to drive this thing called life,
Did not think anyone cared, so I tried to hide,
Today I can think and now I can see,
It's up to me to be the best I can be,
I needed God in my life to see the real me,
He took her hand; he gave her a hug,
He said, "Queen, I made you; I'm your father from above,"
With me, you won't have to beg,
I will give you lite to shine like a star,
Ride with me, I'll be your guide!

My name is Kariem, and I approve this message!

Mikal Bethea

Reflection

Beautiful complexion comprised of silk and cinnamon, full lips glistening.
She's speaking, are you listening?
It's embedded in her gaze, defined amongst her words,
Message to the black man once unheeded finally heard.
Majestic queen requesting an audience,
Ignorant mentalities exceeding her tolerance,
Cloaked in knowledge, understanding etched upon her face,
She shields the king,
Society conspires to erase.
She questions the Trump's, the Bushes', and the Hillary's,
How do you teach the original queen black history?
Intellectually conscious, endorsing fact, never fiction,
The black man is our king, not our affliction.
Propagating righteous, powerful thoughts,
Eradicating the bull stuff your history books taught.
It's time for our people to amalgamate,
Being pro-black doesn't advocate hate.
Loving ourselves without oppressing others, ceasing abrupt denouement of our sisters and brothers, frustration in her eyes, pain in her words,
Message from a queen, once unheeded, finally heard.

Tonya Thetakeover Cherry

A Message to You

God said, "I'll make you a woman,"
A woman of beauty;
A woman of substance, pride, integrity, and love,
Who is worthy of the treasures I have to give you.
A woman who is genuine, a leader, and a queen,
A woman will at times feel pain, learn from it, fight through it, shake it off, and swing out like never before.
This woman is you! Put on your crown!

My name is Kariem, and I approve this message!

Special songs for you:
-Earth Wind and Fire 'Shining Star'
-Raheem DeVaughn 'Queen'

Author's Note

I really enjoyed writing this book. I hope that at least one of my poems touched you. If so, I've accomplished my mission; I've done my job.

I didn't intend on making women seem weak or anything of the sort. But, I do understand that "some" are.

It's nothing to be ashamed of, because all strong people were once weak, just like all smart and intelligent people were once ignorant... And all leaders had to follow at one point in their lives.

But the question is, "Will you take the initiative to do something about your life?" Will you search your soul? I assure you that you'll find out you had way more power than you thought.

Everything I said in this book is the truth, But the truth will only have power in your life if you believe it. Believe, and then act off your belief. You can accomplish anything if you invest your mind. First, you must search your soul!

Please like us on Facebook @Bricks4LifePublishing
Check out our website: www.bricks4lifepublishing.com

Thank you!

www.ingramcontent.com/pod-product-compliance
Lightning Source LLC
Chambersburg PA
CBHW070302100426
42743CB00011B/2318